CHRISTMAS ICONS
COLORING BOOK

HOPE AND LIFE PRESS

First published in 2017 by
HOPE AND LIFE PRESS

Christmas Icons Coloring Book

Copyright © 2017 Hope and Life Press – All rights reserved.

Published by
HOPE AND LIFE PRESS
2312 Chemin Herron #A, Dorval QC, H9S 1C5 Canada; and
P.O. Box 37, East Longmeadow, MA 01028, USA.
http://hopeandlifepress.com
hopeandlifepress@gmail.com

All rights reserved. No part of this work may be reproduced, stored in a retrieval system, or submitted in any form or by any means, electronic, mechanical, photocopying, recording or otherwise, without the prior written permission of the publisher. This book may not be lent, resold, hired out or otherwise disposed of by way of trade in any form of binding or cover other than that in which it is published, without the prior written consent of the published.

Printed in the United States of America.

CONTENTS

CHRISTMAS ICONS COLORING BOOK

Jesus Christ	5
The Annunciation	6
The Nativity – 1	7
Detail of the Nativity	8
The Nativity – 2	9
The Holy Family – 1	10
Baby Jesus in the Manger	11
The Three Kings	12
The Presentation in the Temple	13
The Holy Family – 2	14
Our Lady With the Child Jesus	15
Christ Emmanuel	16
Saint Joseph and Saint Mary	17
Archangel Gabriel	18
Archangel Michael – 1	19
Archangel Michael – 2	20
Guardian Angel	21
The Holy Trinity	22
The Baptism of Jesus Christ	23
The Cross	24
Select Books of Hope and Life Press	25

Jesus Christ

The Annunciation

The Nativity - 1

Detail of the Nativity

THE NATIVITY - 2

The Holy Family – 1

Baby Jesus in the Manger

THE THREE KINGS

The Presentation in the Temple

The Holy Family - 2

Our Lady with the Child Jesus

CHRIST EMMANUEL

Saint Joseph and Saint Mary

ARCHANGEL GABRIEL

Archangel Michael - 1

Archangel Michael - 2

Guardian Angel

THE HOLY TRINITY

THE BAPTISM OF JESUS CHRIST

The Cross

Select Books of Hope and Life Press

  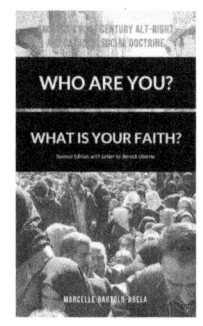  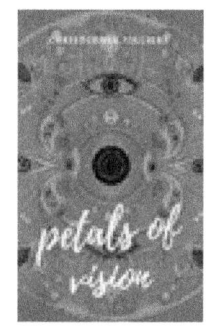

    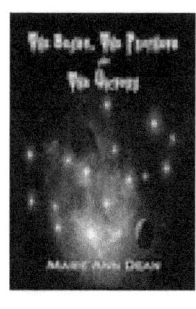

   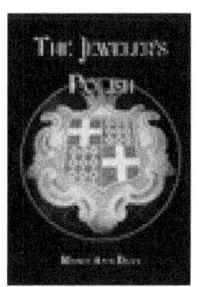

www.ingramcontent.com/pod-product-compliance
Lightning Source LLC
Chambersburg PA
CBHW080416300426
44113CB00015B/2546